Parenting Gen Alpha: Brain Science, Chaos, and Laughter

A Mom's Guide to Raising the Next Gen

SHAHISTA ISMAIL

Copyright © Shahista Ismail
All Rights Reserved.

This book has been self-published with all reasonable efforts taken to make the material error-free by the author. No part of this book shall be used, reproduced in any manner whatsoever without written permission from the author, except in the case of brief quotations embodied in critical articles and reviews.

The Author of this book is solely responsible and liable for its content including but not limited to the views, representations, descriptions, statements, information, opinions and references ["Content"]. The Content of this book shall not constitute or be construed or deemed to reflect the opinion or expression of the Publisher or Editor. Neither the Publisher nor Editor endorse or approve the Content of this book or guarantee the reliability, accuracy or completeness of the Content published herein and do not make any representations or warranties of any kind, express or implied, including but not limited to the implied warranties of merchantability, fitness for a particular purpose. The Publisher and Editor shall not be liable whatsoever for any errors, omissions, whether such errors or omissions result from negligence, accident, or any other cause or claims for loss or damages of any kind, including without limitation, indirect or consequential loss or damage arising out of use, inability to use, or about the reliability, accuracy or sufficiency of the information contained in this book.

Made with ♥ on the Notion Press Platform
www.notionpress.com

DEDICATION

To my wonderful family—my biggest inspiration and greatest joy.
To my children, who teach me new lessons every day with their laughter, curiosity, and boundless energy.
And to my loving husband, whose support, patience, and love make everything possible.
This book is for you.

CONTENTS

ACKNOWLEDGMENTS

This book would not have been possible without the love, encouragement, and support of so many people in my life.
To my husband, thank you for being my rock, my sounding board, and my greatest cheerleader. Your patience and belief in me have been my constant motivation.
To my children, you are my inspiration. Your daily adventures, challenges, and joys have shaped this book more than you know.
To my family and friends, your unwavering support and understanding have carried me through this journey. Thank you for listening, offering advice, and being there every step of the way.
And to all the parents out there, navigating the wonderful and chaotic world of parenting—this book is for you.

PROLOGUE

The Journey Begins – From the Middle Child to Montessori Mom

Hello and welcome to this parenting adventure! I'm Shahista Ismail, founder and director of FloMont World School, where we've made it our mission to combine the best of Montessori education and brain-based teaching practices. I hold a Master's degree in Montessori Teaching and am currently pursuing my PhD in Brain-Based Learning and Teaching. But by far, my most important degree—the one that has taught me the most, challenged me in ways I never imagined, and brought me the greatest joy—is in **parenting**.

I'm a mother of three wonderfully unique children: a 16-year-old daughter, a 9-year-old son, and a 6-year-old son. Parenting them has been the wildest, most fulfilling ride of my life. And though I've spent years studying education, nothing quite prepares you for the reality of raising human beings who come with their own personalities, quirks, and endless demands. My professional qualifications help, but it's the daily, hands-on experience of being their mother that truly shapes me.

But before I dive into how brain science and Montessori education have shaped my approach to parenting, let me take you back to my own childhood—a time when parenting was an entirely different ballgame.

Parenting in My Day: Trial, Error, and Strict Rules

I grew up in a household where parenting was much more... let's say, *traditional*. My parents, like most parents of their generation, didn't have access to books, blogs, or podcasts on child-rearing. There were no fancy theories about brain development or positive discipline. Instead, parenting was often a mix of firm rules, discipline, and, quite honestly, a lot of **trial and error**.

I was the middle child of three siblings (yes, the infamous "middle child"). My older brother bore the brunt of the discipline—he was the one who had to follow the rules to the letter and face the consequences when he didn't. Meanwhile, my younger sister could get away with practically anything. And then there was me, the one who somehow managed to hold it all together, keeping the peace and making sure my parents didn't completely lose their minds.

It's ironic that, even back then, I played the role of the **sane** one. While my brother was getting lectured for staying out too late and my sister was sneaking her way out of chores, I was the steady one, making sure I didn't rock the boat too much. It was a delicate balance, but somehow, I managed to survive the whirlwind of being stuck between two very different siblings.

Learning by Doing: The Unwritten Parenting Rules

Looking back, I realize that my parents did the best they could with the tools they had. They were strict, yes, but they also loved us deeply. And while their methods might not always align with today's approach to parenting, they raised us with values that stuck: respect, hard work, and the understanding that family always comes first.

In many ways, their parenting style was built on instinct and tradition. My parents weren't following any manuals or listening to expert advice on child psychology. They parented the way they had been parented—firmly, with clear expectations and little room for negotiation. But in between the strict rules and chores, there was love. It wasn't always spoken out loud, but it was felt in the way they provided for us, kept us in line, and made sure we stayed on the right path.

Their methods weren't perfect (and whose are?), but they shaped who I am as a person—and as a mother. And though I've taken a more intentional, research-based approach to parenting my own children, I carry with me the lessons I learned from being a child in a household where discipline, structure, and love were all tightly woven together.

From Middle Child to Montessori Mom

As a middle child, I often felt like I was navigating between two worlds—the rule-following, high-expectation world of my older brother, and the carefree, get-away-with-anything world of my younger sister. It's probably why I've developed a keen sense of balance, both as a parent and as an educator.

That sense of balance is something I've poured into my work at FloMont World School, where we focus on creating environments that balance independence with guidance, freedom with structure, and curiosity with responsibility. The Montessori method, which values hands-on learning, respect for the child's pace, and fostering a love of learning, deeply resonates with me—not just as an educator, but as a mother. And let me tell you, as a parent of three wildly different personalities, Montessori principles have saved my sanity more times than I can count.

Why Parenting Is the Greatest Lesson of All

Despite my degrees and professional experience, nothing has taught me more about human development, patience, and resilience than my own children. Parenting is, in every sense, the greatest and most humbling education we can receive. It's a journey where there's no real handbook (even though I'm writing this book!), and every day presents new lessons, challenges, and joys.

Raising my children has been the most fulfilling and, at times, exhausting adventure of my life. Watching them grow—each with their unique strengths, weaknesses, and quirks—reminds me that parenting is not about creating perfect children or following a specific formula. It's about **celebrating who they are**, helping them develop into the best version of themselves, and learning to love them through every twist and turn of the journey.

As I've juggled my full-time role as the director of a school, pursued my PhD, and navigated the day-to-day chaos of motherhood, my children have been my constant source of joy and inspiration. They remind me that time, while precious, is not measured in hours spent together but, in the moments, we make count. I may not be the mother who is home all the time, but the time we share is filled with love, laughter, and deep connection.

For Every Parent Out There

To all the parents reading this, know this: **you are enough**. You don't need to be perfect, and your children don't expect you to be. They love you for showing up, for trying, and for being there when it counts. Parenting is a journey for both parent and child, and we all grow together.

As you move through this book, you'll find brain-based insights, practical strategies, and, hopefully, some laughs along the way. My hope is that this book helps you navigate the messy, wonderful world of parenting, but also that it reminds you to celebrate your children for who they are—unique, imperfect, and full of potential.

Welcome to the parenting journey. Let's embrace it together.

Chapter 1

Neuroscience for the Sleep-Deprived

How Your Kid's Brain Works

Let me tell you, nothing says "brain science" like the chaos of parenting three kids at very different stages of life. As a mother of a teen who knows everything, a nine-year-old who constantly questions everything, and a six-year-old who thinks bedtime is a conspiracy, I've had my fair share of neuro-experiments happening right under my roof.

But here's the good news: understanding how your child's brain works can not only help you stay sane—it might even make you laugh at the things that used to drive you up the wall.

Let's dive in.

The Brain in Action: Why Your Six-Year-Old Won't Stop Moving

When my youngest, a whirlwind of energy and questions, turned six, I realized I'd need more than coffee to keep up. I needed to know "why" he could ask 43 questions before breakfast but still struggle to tie his shoes. The answer? His "prefrontal cortex"—the part of the brain responsible for logic, focus, and self-control—is still under construction. Think of it as a slow Wi-Fi connection. It's trying its best, but things are going to buffer for a while.

This explains why a simple request like "please put on your shoes" can somehow lead to a 15-minute investigation of why the dog's tongue is blue. The secret? Their little brains are curious and wired for exploration. It's frustrating, yes, but that curiosity is exactly what helps their brains develop. They're building neural connections faster than my Wi-Fi drops during a Zoom meeting, and even though it can feel like chaos, that's how learning happens.

Mom Hack: Instead of getting frustrated, I've learned to roll with it. When my youngest launches into his 34th question of the day, I use it as a chance to build his critical thinking. "Why do you think the dog's tongue is blue?" I ask, turning the interrogation back on him. It keeps the conversation going, buys me time, and sometimes, we both end up learning something.

The Teenage Brain: A Work in Progress

Ah, the teenage brain. If there's ever a time when brain science becomes essential, it's during the teenage years. My 16-year-old thinks she knows more about life than Google. And, in a way, she's right. The teenage brain is going through some serious rewiring. The "amygdala", the brain's emotional centre, is in overdrive, while the "prefrontal cortex"—remember, that logical, reasoning part? — is still catching up.

This means that when my teen tells me, "Mom, you just don't get it!" (for the fifth time that day), she's not being dramatic; she's being a teen. Her brain is running on emotions. And guess what? Her brain is right on schedule. Neuroscience tells us that a teen's brain is wired for risk-taking, pushing boundaries, and craving independence. It's all part of preparing them for adulthood (though it sometimes feels like it's preparing me for an early midlife crisis).

Mom Hack: When emotions are running high, I take a deep breath and remember that my teen's brain is just doing its job—making things harder for me so she can grow into a functioning adult. So instead of diving into the emotional chaos with her, I try to model calmness. Easier said than done? Absolutely. But hey, brain science reminds me I'm the adult here (even if I don't always feel like it).

Middle Child Syndrome (and the Neuroscience Behind It)

Then there's my nine-year-old, living in the sweet spot between chaos and curiosity. Middle children get a bad rap, but here's where brain science comes to the rescue. At nine, his brain is transitioning from the more emotional, impulsive stages of early childhood into what I like to call the "mini adult" phase. His "hippocampus"—the part of the brain involved in memory—is more developed, which explains why he can recite every stat about his favourite football player but still forgets to put his dirty socks in the hamper.

At this age, kids are starting to develop more complex thinking skills, but they still need structure and guidance. They're learning how to balance emotional responses with logical thinking. As a middle child, he's also navigating the tricky territory of independence and sibling rivalry, which is a whole separate chapter in the book of parenting chaos.

Mom Hack: I give my nine-year-old more responsibility while keeping a close eye on his emotional needs. I find that letting him "teach" his younger sibling something helps boost his confidence and reinforces his learning. Plus, it keeps the sibling squabbles at bay—for at least five minutes.

The Science Behind the Chaos

What I've learned from raising three kids in these wildly different stages is that their brains are in constant flux. Understanding the brain's development has saved my sanity more times than I can count. Instead of seeing their behaviours as frustrating, I now view them as brain-driven milestones. Each stage, from the toddler years to the teenage years, is guided by the incredible journey of brain development. Knowing that helps me keep things in perspective—and occasionally find humour in the madness.

If you, like me, have ever found yourself hiding in the bathroom just to get a moment of peace, here's some good news: The chaos is brain approved. It means your kids are learning, growing, and developing into their future selves. So, next time your six-year-old asks you why the sky is blue for the 100th time, take a deep breath, smile, and remember—you're raising a brain in progress.

And hey, that's something to be proud of!

Chapter 2

Surviving the Emotional Roller Coaster

From Toddler Tantrums to Teen Meltdowns

Let's be honest, parenting is a little like running an emotional obstacle course. One minute your six-year-old is crying because the dog looked at him "funny," and the next, your sixteen-year-old is in full-blown existential crisis mode because life is just **so unfair.** Meanwhile, your nine-year-old? He's calm—for now. (Middle-child zen, right?) But you know it's only a matter of time before he launches into a speech about how you never listen to him.

As much as we'd love to think it's all just a phase, the truth is, their brains are to blame. The emotional roller coaster is a necessary part of development, thanks to the complex way their brains grow and mature. But understanding that doesn't necessarily make it easier when you're in the trenches. So, buckle up, because we're diving into the science of emotions, meltdowns, and how to keep your own sanity intact.

The Six-Year-Old's Emotional Brain: It's Like a Tiny Volcano

Let's start with my youngest. He's six, which, according to brain science, means he's emotionally unpredictable—basically a tiny volcano that could erupt at any moment. His **amygdala**, which controls emotional responses, is working overtime. On the flip side, his **prefrontal cortex** (that trusty logic centre we discussed in Chapter 1) is still, well, trying to catch up. This means emotions can, and often do, hijack his brain.

The result? A lot of tears. Over everything. From socks that "feel weird" to the unfairness of the sun setting before he's finished playing. To his brain, these are actual crises. His emotional responses aren't just dramatic for the sake of drama—they're real to him because his brain hasn't yet mastered the art of **self-regulation**.

Mom Hack: When the volcano erupts, instead of rushing to fix it, I let the storm pass. With younger kids, giving them space to express emotions is key to helping their brains

learn how to regulate over time. I try to name the emotion for him, "I see you're frustrated because your sock doesn't feel right." It sounds simple, but just naming the feeling can help the brain process it. Then, I offer two simple choices: "Do you want to wear the blue socks or the red ones?" Two choices. Not five. Because I value my sanity.

Real-Life Example: Last week, my son had a full meltdown because his favourite toy car wasn't racing fast enough. His **amygdala** was clearly calling the shots. After 10 minutes of tears and dramatic declarations of never playing again, I offered him two choices: "Do you want to fix the car or switch to another game?" He chose to fix the car, meltdown over. The **prefrontal cortex** is slow, but it's learning.

The Nine-Year-Old: Mastering the "Big Feelings"

Now, my nine-year-old's brain is slightly more evolved than his younger sibling's. He's starting to understand his emotions a little better, but that doesn't mean we're free from drama. At this age, kids are developing more emotional intelligence, but they're still grappling with **"big feelings."** These feelings can seem overwhelming to them, whether it's disappointment, frustration, or that deep sense of injustice that occurs when they lose a board game (even if they totally cheated).

What's happening here? His **hippocampus** is working hard to store memories, and his amygdala is still loud, but the prefrontal cortex is finally coming online a bit more. He's more capable of **emotional regulation**, but not always. Hence, the occasional sulk fest after a sibling gets more screen time.

Mom Hack: With kids this age, empathy is your secret weapon. I've found that reflecting his feelings back to him helps lower the emotional stakes. When he's upset, instead of rushing to calm him down or fix things, I say, "I can see you're really frustrated right now." It doesn't stop the frustration, but it helps him feel understood.

And once he feels heard, the door opens to problem-solving. I call it "emotional judo"—use their emotions to guide them into calm instead of fighting against them.

Real-Life Example: My nine-year-old, aka the board game king, had a major emotional blowout when his sister beat him at Monopoly. After five minutes of huffing and puffing, I leaned in with my emotional judo move: "It's hard when you play so well and don't win, isn't it?" He nodded. I followed with, "What can we do differently next time to make it fair?" In that moment, the conversation shifted from emotional chaos to critical thinking. And yes, he demanded a rematch.

The Teenage Brain: Welcome to the Emotional Roller Coaster

Then there's my teenager. Sixteen years old, full of confidence one-minute, existential dread the next. The truth is, her brain is in the midst of a major overhaul, much like a renovation project that isn't going according to plan. The **prefrontal cortex** (responsible for decision-making and impulse control) is still under construction, while the **amygdala** is doing its best impression of a teenager at a rock concert—loud, emotional, and not always making sense.

Teenagers feel everything intensely. Everything is either amazing or horrible—there's no in-between. This is why a simple disagreement about curfew can turn into a full-blown emotional standoff. It's not that teens are deliberately dramatic (okay, sometimes they are), but their brains are wired to be **hyper-emotional** during these years.

Mom Hack: When the emotional waves hit, it's tempting to meet fire with fire. Instead, I try to stay cool and give her space. I acknowledge her feelings without trying to fix them. "I get that you're upset, and that's okay. Let's talk when we're both calmer." This buys both of us time to get the prefrontal cortex back in control. Also, if you can slip in a little humour, it helps de-escalate the situation. But be careful - teens can sniff out sarcasm like a bloodhound.

Real-Life Example: The other day, my sixteen-year-old went into full meltdown mode over—you guessed it—her phone. Apparently, asking her to put it away during dinner was an act of aggression. She stormed off, and instead of chasing after her, I stayed calm (on the outside, at least). Later, when things cooled down, I told her, "You know, I used to survive without a phone at the table. It was tough, but I made it." She laughed. Conflict over, for now.

Brain Science: Why Emotional Ups and Downs Are Normal

If you're feeling like an emotional referee some days, congratulations—you are. But here's the thing: **emotional ups and**

downs are a normal part of brain development. Your child's brain is in constant flux, and their ability to regulate emotions depends on what stage of brain development they're in. Toddlers and young kids have brains that are all amygdala, little logic. By the time they hit adolescence, they're dealing with hormonal changes and a brain that's rewiring itself for adulthood. It's a messy, beautiful process. Your job isn't to control the chaos—it's to help them navigate it. By understanding that their emotional outbursts are often driven by brain biology, not just bad behavior, you can step back, take a deep breath, and offer support without losing your cool (most of the time).

Mom Hack: The Pause Button

Before we wrap up, here's one more tip that has saved me countless times: **Hit the pause button**. When emotions are high—whether it's a toddler tantrum or a teen meltdown—pause before you react. Give yourself and your child a moment to let the emotional storm pass. During that pause, their brain gets a chance to catch up, and so does yours.

Chapter 3

The Art of Positive Discipline

Train Their Brain, Not Just Their Behaviour

Let's start with a confession: before I had kids, I used to think that discipline was simple. I'd just lay down the rules, they'd follow them, and we'd all live in harmony like a well-organized Pinterest board. Then, my first child turned two and gave me my first real taste of rebellion. Fast forward to today, and with three kids—ages 16, 9, and 6—I can say with certainty that discipline is anything but straightforward. It's more like a game of Whack-a-Mole, but with emotions and tiny people you're legally obligated to love.

Discipline, however, doesn't have to be a constant battle of wills. As I've learned (through much trial and error, and a lot of deep breaths), positive discipline is the key. It's not about control or punishment but about training your child's brain to make better decisions, handle emotions, and grow into a reasonably functioning human. Sounds easy, right? Spoiler: it's not. But it is possible, and it can even be kind of fun when you understand how your child's brain works.

Why Positive Discipline Works: A Brain-Based Approach

Positive discipline aligns with brain science because it focuses on teaching, not punishing. When kids misbehave, it's often because their brain hasn't yet developed the skills needed to manage big emotions, impulses, or complex social situations. The goal of positive discipline is to help them learn these skills rather than just stop the behaviour in the moment.

Here's the deal: when you yell, punish, or react out of frustration, your child's **amygdala** (emotional brain) goes into overdrive. This triggers the fight-or-flight response, which means they stop thinking logically and react emotionally. But when you use calm, positive discipline, you engage their **prefrontal cortex** —the part of the brain responsible for decision-making and self-regulation.

In other words, discipline isn't about winning a power struggle; it's about helping your child's brain grow.

The 6-Year-Old and the Case of the Vanishing Patience

Let's start with my six-year-old. If you've ever tried reasoning with a six-year-old in the middle of a supermarket meltdown, you know that logic and calm are nowhere to be found. Six-year-olds live in the moment, and their **prefrontal cortex** is still in its infancy. Impulse control? Hardly. Patience? Rare. Instant gratification? Oh, yes.

The other day, my youngest had a meltdown because I told him he couldn't have a popsicle right before dinner. His response? **Full-body despair**. Arms flailing, tears streaming, and dramatic declarations of eternal hunger. My natural reaction was to tell him to "stop it," but then I remembered that his emotional brain was in charge at that moment. No amount of reasoning was going to work until we calmed the storm.

Mom Hack (Positive Discipline in Action): I got down to his level, kept my voice calm (because losing it would only escalate things), and used what brain science calls **"connect before correct."** I empathized with his frustration: "I know, you really want that popsicle right now." Once I saw a flicker of recognition in his eyes (he felt understood!), I followed with a simple choice: "You can have the popsicle after dinner, or you can help me set the table." This gave him control—something kids this age crave—while guiding him back to calm behaviour. Did he help set the table? No. But he did stop crying, and that felt like a win.

The Nine-Year-Old and the Quest for Fairness

My nine-year-old is all about fairness. He has a built-in justice system, and he's ready to enforce it at all times. Whether it's who got the biggest slice of cake or why his sister got 10 extra minutes of screen time, fairness is his hill to die on. His brain, being more developed than his younger siblings, is starting to grasp concepts like fairness, but his **prefrontal cortex** still isn't fully equipped to handle it calmly all the time.

When he felt wronged last week (because his sister got the last turn on a video game), he stomped, slammed doors, and declared that life was "soooo unfair." Again, my initial reaction was to tell him to calm down (which, fun fact, never works). Instead, I turned to positive discipline.

Mom Hack: Positive discipline teaches that we need to **validate** their feelings before we correct their behaviour. So, I acknowledged his sense of injustice: "It doesn't feel good when it seems like things aren't fair, does it?" This gave him the space to express his feelings without escalating the situation. Then I set a clear boundary: "I understand you're upset, but slamming doors isn't okay. You can either talk to your sister about taking turns, or we can take a break and talk about it later."

In that moment, he chose to storm off (again, winning isn't always about immediate results). But guess what? Ten minutes later, he came back, much calmer, and we were able to talk it out. His **prefrontal cortex** needed time to catch up and giving him that space helped him regulate his emotions.

The Teenager and the Battle of Independence

Ah, the teenage brain—an evolving masterpiece of hormones, independence, and emotional fireworks. My 16-year-old is at that stage where she desperately wants to be treated like an adult but also still asks me for snacks at midnight. The teenage **prefrontal cortex** is under major reconstruction, which means logical decision-making and impulse control aren't exactly top tier. Mix in a raging **amygdala** (emotion central), and you've got a recipe for drama.

Last week, she came home late from the neighbourhood library. She insisted she needed her "space" to study. She also insisted on going there on her own. We'd agreed on a 4 p.m. curfew. I was worried sick till she got back wondering if she would be alright finding her way home, but she strolled in at 6:30 p.m with an attitude like she'd just returned from a United Nations summit. My immediate reaction was to lay down the law, but again, brain science reminded me that this wasn't just about rules—it was about helping her learn to manage responsibility.

Mom Hack (Positive Discipline for Teens): With teens, it's all about **mutual respect** and setting clear consequences. So, instead of yelling (tempting as it was), I calmly told her, "I get that you were at the library, but we agreed on a curfew, and you broke it." Then I asked, "What do you think would be a fair consequence?" This made her think critically (engaging that **prefrontal cortex**) rather than reacting emotionally.

To my surprise, she suggested losing her weekend privileges if it happened again. By involving her in the consequence-setting process, I gave her ownership over her behaviour. And the best part? No yelling, no tears—just a calm conversation that helped her understand the connection between actions and consequences.

Positive Discipline Techniques that Align with Brain Science

Here are some techniques that have saved me from countless parenting meltdowns (my own and my kids'):

1. **Connect Before You Correct**: When emotions are high, your child's brain is not in a position to listen or learn. Acknowledge their feelings first, even if you don't agree with them. This calms the emotional brain (amygdala) and makes them more receptive to guidance.

2. **Choices, Not Commands**: Give your child options instead of issuing orders. "Do you want to put your toys away now or in five minutes?" This activates their decision-making brain (prefrontal cortex) and gives them a sense of control, reducing power struggles.

3. **Natural Consequences**: Letting kids experience the natural consequences of their actions can be a powerful teacher. If they refuse to wear a jacket, they'll feel cold. Instead of lecturing, let them learn from the experience, and next time, they'll think twice.

4. **Time-Ins, Not Time-Outs**: Instead of isolating them when they misbehave, bring them closer. A "time-in" allows them to cool down with your support, helping them regulate their emotions. It reinforces that you're there for them even when things go wrong.

5. **Teach Problem-Solving:** When conflicts arise (like sibling squabbles), resist the urge to fix it for them. Instead, guide them through solving it themselves. This builds resilience and teaches them to manage conflicts independently, using both logic and empathy.

The Brain and Discipline: Growing Together

At the end of the day, discipline isn't about controlling your child's behaviour. It's about helping them grow. Every meltdown, every argument, every "life isn't fair!" moment is an opportunity for their brain to learn and develop. Sure, it's exhausting. And yes, sometimes you'll want to hide in the bathroom with a pint of ice cream. But positive discipline is an investment—not just in their future, but in your relationship with them.

By understanding how their brain works, you can discipline in a way that strengthens both their self-control and your sanity. So next time the inevitable chaos erupts, remember it's all part of the process. And somewhere in the middle of it, you're both learning.

Chapter 4

Building Resilience in a Digital World

Can They Handle Screen Time Without Meltdowns?

Let's face it: screen time is the modern-day Pandora's box of parenting. What started as a few minutes of harmless cartoons on a tablet has turned into a full-blown, unavoidable part of daily life. In our house, screens are everywhere: the TV, the tablet, the phone, the computer. Sometimes, it feels like I'm running a mini-tech support office. My six-year-old can navigate YouTube better than I can, my nine-year-old uses Google to argue more effectively, and my sixteen-year-old can carry out an entire social life through her phone without ever needing to leave her room.

As a parent who's trying to keep their children's brains healthy (and their meltdowns to a minimum), I've found myself walking the tightrope of balancing screen time and real-life experiences. And trust me, it's no easy feat.

But, once again, brain science comes to the rescue. By understanding how screen time impacts their developing brains, I've found ways to build resilience in my kids, so they can handle the digital world without turning into tiny (or not-so-tiny) zombies. And yes, that means fewer meltdowns when it's time to *turn off the tablet*—something I once thought was impossible.

What Screen Time Does to the Brain: The Good, the Bad, and the Meltdown-Prone

Before we dive into the tactics, let's look at what screen time actually does to a child's brain. This is important because, spoiler alert, screens aren't inherently evil. They just need to be handled with care—like chocolate or those white couches you've always wanted but never dared to buy.

When kids are engaged in screens—whether it's a game, a video, or endless scrolling—their **dopamine** levels (the "feel good" chemical) surge. That's why it's so hard to pry them away from the screen without tears and tantrums. Their brains are literally craving more of that dopamine hit. It's like trying to get them to step away from an all-you-can-eat candy buffet.

But here's where it gets tricky: too much screen time can overload their **prefrontal cortex**, the part of the brain responsible for decision-making and impulse control. That's why, after hours of screen time, your normally sweet six-year-old turns into a grumpy gremlin who can't handle being told "no." Their brain is on digital overload.

However, it's not all bad news. Screens, when used wisely, can offer a lot of benefits—educational games, creative apps, and even a little downtime can be good for the brain. The key is balance, and that's where resilience comes in.

The Six-Year-Old and the Battle of the Tablet

Let's start with my youngest. He loves his tablet like it's a long-lost sibling. I get it—it's colourful, engaging, and full of videos that somehow keep his attention longer than anything I could say. But the problem comes when it's time to turn it off.

Last week, I told him that his 30 minutes of tablet time were up. His reaction? You'd think I had just announced the end of civilization. He threw himself on the couch, face down, kicking and crying as if his life depended on watching one more episode of whatever strange cartoon YouTube had recommended next.

Here's where brain science helped me understand the meltdown. His brain was hooked on the dopamine high, and taking the tablet away was like pulling candy from a sugar-crazed toddler. So, instead of reacting emotionally (which was hard, because trust me, I wanted to yell), I used a positive discipline technique called **"transitions."** This technique gives his brain time to adjust to the idea of stopping the activity, preventing that dopamine crash.

Mom Hack (Building Resilience in Little Ones): I've started giving my six-year-old **transition cues**. Instead of yanking the tablet away after 30 minutes, I say, "You have 5 more minutes of tablet time, and then we're going to color a picture together." This not only helps him mentally prepare for the end of screen time, but it also gives him something positive to look forward to—engaging his **prefrontal cortex** and making the transition smoother.

Real-Life Example: Last week, I used the transition strategy, and when the timer went off, I said, "Okay, buddy, it's time to put the tablet down. Let's go pick out some crayons." He groaned a little but put the tablet down without the full-body drama. Was it a perfect, angelic moment? No. But there were no tears, and I'll take that as a victory.

The Nine-Year-Old: Master Negotiator of Screen Time

My nine-year-old is a tech enthusiast in training. He loves Minecraft, coding games, and anything that lets him build virtual worlds. And he's clever about it. He'll negotiate screen time like a seasoned lawyer. "But, Mom, if I just finish this one building, I'll stop," he says, already knowing that "just one more minute" means at least twenty more.

Here's the thing: nine-year-olds are starting to develop the **executive function** skills (like planning, focus, and time management) that will help them become responsible screen users. But they're not there yet. So, while he understands that there's a limit, his brain still needs some external support to actually stop when the time is up.

Mom Hack (Positive Discipline for the Negotiator): Instead of fighting the endless negotiations, I turn the responsibility over to him using **"self-monitoring tools."** We use a kitchen timer, and I let him set it. "You can play for 30 minutes, and when the timer goes off, it's time to stop." By giving him control over the timer, I'm helping his brain learn how to manage time and making him responsible for the transition.

Real-Life Example: A few days ago, we tried the timer trick. He set it himself, and when the timer beeped, he actually turned off the game without the usual haggling. I won't lie—my jaw dropped. He said, "Well, I did set the timer." Brain science for the win! Giving him control helped engage his prefrontal cortex, and he felt empowered to follow through.

The Teenager and the Phone Epidemic

Now, let's talk about my teenager. I swear, her phone is glued to her hand. She's either texting, scrolling, or Face Timing her friends. If you've ever tried to get a teenager off their phone, you know it's like trying to remove gum from your hair—it's messy, frustrating, and you're never quite sure how it got there in the first place.

The teenage brain is wired for social connection. The **prefrontal cortex** is still under construction, which means impulse control is a work in progress. Add in a constant stream of notifications, likes, and social media dopamine hits, and you've got a perfect storm of phone addiction.

Mom Hack (Building Digital Resilience in Teens): I've learned that with teens, it's not about banning screens (because, let's face it, that's impossible). Instead, it's about **setting boundaries and helping them self-regulate.** We have phone-free times in our house—dinner, family movie night, and an hour before bed. We also have a rule where her phone charges outside her room at night, so she's not tempted to scroll until 2 a.m.

Real-Life Example: Last week, she rolled her eyes when I reminded her to put the phone in the charging station before bed. "Mom, I'm 16. I know when to sleep." But sure enough, the next morning, she admitted, "I actually slept better without my phone buzzing all night." I resisted the urge to say "I told you so" (barely) and instead used it as a moment to reinforce the idea that screen limits are good for her brain.

Positive Discipline Techniques for Building Digital Resilience

Here are some tried-and-tested techniques that have helped me manage screen time with my kids, without the meltdowns:

1. **Set Clear Boundaries**: Establish rules around screen time that everyone understands, like "no screens during dinner" or "phones charge outside the bedroom at night." Consistency is key. When kids know the rules, their brains are more likely to accept them.

2. **Use Transition Warnings**: Giving kids a five-minute warning before the screen goes off helps their brain prepare for the change. Sudden stops trigger emotional reactions, but transitions give their brain time to adjust.

3. **Encourage Self-Monitoring**: Use timers, clocks, or even apps that track screen usage to help kids become more aware of how long they've been on a device. This builds their ability to self-regulate and engages the prefrontal cortex.

4. **Offer Alternatives**: When screen time ends, have a fun alternative ready, whether it's a family activity, a creative project, or even just a snack together. This helps distract from the dopamine crash and redirects their attention.

5. **Model Healthy Screen Habits**: Let's be real, kids learn by watching us. If we're glued to our phones, they'll notice. I've started practicing phone-free time myself, and when I do, it sets a good example. Plus, it's good for my brain too!

Resilience in a Digital World

In today's world, screens aren't going anywhere, but that doesn't mean we have to let them take over our kids' lives (or our sanity). By building resilience - both emotional and cognitive - we can help our kids navigate the digital world without losing themselves in it.

As parents, our goal isn't to eliminate screens; it's to teach our kids how to use them wisely, manage their own time, and balance their digital lives with real-world experiences. And trust me, with a little brain science and a lot of patience, it's possible to do this without constant battles.

Chapter 5

Siblings, Squabbles, and Neuroscience

Why Your Kids Argue, and How to Stay Sane

Let me paint you a picture: It's dinner time. The table is set, the food is ready, and I'm just about to experience 30 seconds of peace. Then, without warning, my teenage daughter decides to lovingly (or so she claims) pat her 9-year-old brother on the head. He flinches like she's set his hair on fire, and before I can blink, my 6-year-old, sensing chaos, jumps in with a well-placed shove. Suddenly, I'm not eating dinner anymore. I'm the referee in a WWE match, complete with shouting, accusations of "he started it," and one very indignant teenager claiming, "They never treat me with respect!"

If this sounds familiar, welcome to the wonderful world of sibling dynamics. While you may feel like your house is in a perpetual state of sibling warfare, the truth is, there's a lot of brain science at work here (and a lot of patience-testing, too). Understanding why your kids fight—and why they seem to enjoy it—can help you survive the madness with your sanity mostly intact.

Why Do They Fight? A Brain Science Breakdown

Sibling squabbles are not just about who gets the bigger slice of pizza (though, let's be honest, that's part of it). Their brains are wired to compete for attention, control, and even resources—things that go back to our most primal instincts. Each child, with their unique brain development stage, has their own "agenda" during these fights, which is why it feels like they're all playing different games and you're the only one trying to keep score.

The 6-Year-Old Instigator: At six, my youngest operates mostly from his **amygdala**—the emotional, impulse-driven part of the brain. His **prefrontal cortex** (responsible for impulse control and logic) is still developing, which means self-regulation is, well, not his strong suit. When he sees an opportunity to stir the pot, he jumps in because it's exciting. He's not thinking about the consequences—he's thinking about the immediate rush of attention, and let's face it, a little chaos.

The 9-Year-Old Trigger: My nine-year-old, on the other hand, is starting to develop a stronger prefrontal cortex, but his **sense of justice** is highly developed. He's the type who believes in fairness, and when things feel out of balance (say, his sister patting his head like he's a puppy), his brain goes into overdrive. His **amygdala** takes over, and just like that, he's triggered into action. What started as a simple head pat is now a full-scale invasion of his personal space, and he must defend his honour.

The Teenage Instigator 2.0: Then there's my 16-year-old. Ah, the beauty of the teenage brain, where the **amygdala** is still running the show and the **prefrontal cortex** is on its extended lunch break. She enjoys teasing her brothers because it gives her a sense of control and—let's be honest—it's entertaining. The drama she creates is like her own personal soap opera, except she's the star, director, and producer. But here's the kicker: when her brothers retaliate, her amygdala goes into full-on victim mode. "They don't respect me!" she cries, all while conveniently forgetting she lit the fuse in the first place.

Why It Gets Physical (and What You Can Do About It)

The physical aspect of these squabbles often starts with the **six-year-old** because, frankly, he's still learning how to manage big emotions with his small body. When he feels threatened, excited, or even just bored, his brain's impulse control (or lack thereof) kicks in, and the easiest way to respond is with his hands. Of course, his **fight-or-flight** response tells him that shoving his older brother is a great idea, even if it rarely ends well for him.

Mom Hack (for Physical Instigators): With younger kids, it's important to teach **replacement behaviours** for their physical impulses. For example, I've started teaching my 6-year-old to use words instead of hands. Easier said than done, right? But instead of saying, "Stop hitting your brother!" (which doesn't engage his thinking brain), I say, "Tell your brother why you're upset." This helps build his **prefrontal cortex**, giving him the tools he needs to express frustration without a fist.

Real-Life Example: The other day, my youngest was about to lunge at his brother over who got to sit in the coveted "recliner chair" (you know, the only chair in the house that seems to matter). I jumped in with a quick, "Tell him why you want that chair so much." Instead of the usual shove, he paused (I could almost see his brain working) and said, "Because it's the best chair and I always sit on it!" His brother, in a rare moment of mercy, said, "Okay, you can have it." A win for positive brain development and my sanity.

Handling the Easily Triggered Child

Now, my nine-year-old is a little more complex. He's got the impulse control of someone trying not to eat the last cookie in the jar—he tries, but the temptation is just too strong. His **amygdala** gets triggered by any perceived unfairness, and before he knows it, he's reacting. The good news is, his brain is ready for more complex problem-solving, but he still needs guidance.

Mom Hack (for the Easily Triggered): For my 9-year-old, we've started using **brain breaks**. When I see him getting worked up, I say, "Let's take a break and breathe." This calms down his amygdala and lets his prefrontal cortex catch up. Once he's calm, we talk about what happened and how he can respond differently next time. This helps him build resilience over time and shows him how to manage his triggers.

Real-Life Example: Last week, his sister patted his head (again) at the dinner table. I could see the rage building behind his eyes. Before he could explode, I said, "Brain break! Let's take a deep breath." He glared at me but then, to my surprise, actually took a breath. We defused the situation before it turned into a scene from a bad reality show. Progress, people. Progress.

How to Handle the Teenager Who Loves to Stir the Pot

Teenagers, as we know, have the unique ability to cause chaos and then act like they've been wronged. My daughter loves to play the "poor me" card after teasing her brothers to the brink of insanity. Her

prefrontal cortex is under construction, but she's fully capable of understanding how her actions lead to consequences—she just prefers to act like they don't.

Mom Hack (for the Drama Queen): With teens, it's all about **logical consequences**. I don't lecture her on how teasing her brothers is wrong (though, trust me, I'm tempted). Instead, I say, "If you want respect, you have to show respect." Then I let her experience the natural consequences. If she winds her brothers up, she's the one who loses privileges (like her beloved phone) because respect goes both ways. This approach forces her to engage her prefrontal cortex and think about how her actions affect others.

Real-Life Example: At dinner last week, she did her usual head-pat routine on her brother, and when he reacted, she wailed about how unfair they are to her. Instead of jumping into the drama, I calmly said, "Looks like the phone is on break tonight. You can earn it back by showing respect to your brothers." The look on her face was priceless. She grumbled but didn't touch their heads for the rest of the evening.

Positive Discipline Techniques for Sibling Rivalry

Here are a few tools that have helped me keep the peace (or at least minimize the battles) between my kids:

1. **Teach Emotional Awareness:** Help your kids name their emotions during fights. When they're yelling, I say, "You seem really frustrated. Can you tell me why?" Naming the emotion helps calm the brain's emotional centre and opens the door to problem-solving.

2. **Encourage Problem-Solving:** Instead of jumping in to referee every fight, I guide my kids through solving it themselves. "What do you think we can do to make this fair?" is a go-to phrase. This builds their **executive function skills** and teaches them to negotiate and compromise.

3. **Set Clear Boundaries and Consequences:** Everyone in our house knows that physical fighting is not allowed. If it happens, there are clear consequences, like losing privileges or having to apologize and make amends. Consistency is key.

4. **Model Respect:** I try (emphasis on *try*) to model the behaviour I want to see. When my kids argue, I show them how to listen and respond respectfully. It doesn't always work, but when they see me handle conflict calmly, it plants the seed.

5. **Use Positive Reinforcement:** When they manage to get along (even for five minutes), I make a big deal out of it. "Look at how well you two are playing together! Great job!" This

reinforces the behaviour I want to see and encourages more peaceful interactions.

Why It's All (Mostly) Normal

Sibling rivalry is one of the most frustrating parts of parenting, but here's the good news: sibling rivalry is completely normal, and it's even a necessary part of your kids' development. As annoying as the constant bickering can be, it helps them learn important life skills like conflict resolution, negotiation, and even empathy. Their brains are still figuring out how to manage emotions, assert independence, and balance fairness. Your job isn't to stop the fighting entirely (though wouldn't that be nice?), but to guide them through it in a way that helps their brains grow.

Sibling rivalry isn't just a byproduct of having more than one kid—it's a natural, often inevitable part of how children's brains develop. It may seem like they're always fighting over toys, attention, or who gets to sit in the *special* chair (which no one cared about yesterday), but beneath the surface, their little brains are learning valuable skills. Let's break it down:

1. Competition for Resources

At its core, sibling rivalry is rooted in a natural, evolutionary instinct—

competing for resources. In caveman days, those resources might have been food or parental protection, but now it's attention, praise, and yes, even control of the remote. In a household with multiple kids, each child feels a subconscious need to secure their "place" in the family hierarchy. Even though they may not understand it, they're competing for their share of your attention, which to them feels like one of life's most valuable resources.

Brain Science Insight: When your kids are fighting for your attention, their **amygdala** (the emotional brain) is firing off signals that say, "This is important! I need to win this!" This is why their reactions can seem so intense—they're driven by an emotional need to feel seen and valued. Their fights may look like battles over toys or who gets the last cookie, but they're really about their desire for your attention, affection, and approval.

2. Development of Social Skills

Sibling fights are a training ground for future social interactions. When your kids argue, negotiate, and (eventually) resolve their conflicts, they're practicing essential life skills like empathy, patience, and compromise. While it might sound strange, these constant squabbles are helping their brains wire the circuits that will allow them to manage relationships outside of the family—whether with friends, classmates, or eventually co-workers.

Brain Science Insight: The constant back-and-forth teaches them emotional regulation. When your 6-year-old throws a toy at his brother, and you step in to guide him through expressing his feelings verbally, you're teaching his **prefrontal cortex** (the logic and reasoning center) how to regulate impulses. This is a long-term project—his brain will take years to fully develop those skills—but every squabble and resolution is building those neural pathways.

3. Learning Boundaries

Kids are still learning where their personal boundaries are—and what better way to figure that out than by testing them on siblings? The pushing, poking, and patting on the head (looking at you, teenager!) are all ways of experimenting with how far they can go before someone pushes back. They're figuring out what makes other people upset, where the line is, and what happens when they cross it.

Brain Science Insight: When your child invades their sibling's personal space (or toys), they're exploring social boundaries, and their brain is processing the results of these interactions. Every time their sibling yells, "Get out of my room!" or, "Stop touching me!" it's feedback that helps them learn what's socially acceptable. Their

prefrontal cortex is slowly piecing together that cause-and-effect relationship, but it's still developing, which is why this process can take, well, years.

4. The Power Struggle

Let's not forget that sibling fights often revolve around control—who's in charge, who gets to make the rules, who has the most influence in the family dynamic. These little power struggles are more than just bickering—they're helping kids learn how to assert themselves and handle leadership roles (or follow others' lead) in a group setting.

Brain Science Insight: The **amygdala**, that emotional and impulsive part of the brain, fuels these power struggles. Kids are learning how to manage their desires to be in control, while also working through the frustration that comes from not always getting their way. The more their **prefrontal cortex** develops, the better they'll get at handling these power struggles calmly. But during childhood, especially in early years, they're still learning how to channel these impulses into positive leadership skills—without needing to physically tackle their siblings to prove a point.

5. Sibling Rivalry as a Cognitive and Emotional Workout

Sibling rivalry, as frustrating as it is, acts like a workout for their brains.

Every time they argue, negotiate, and (hopefully) make up, their brain is processing all kinds of valuable emotional and cognitive information. Each conflict is an opportunity for them to understand their emotions, learn how to handle frustration, and practice empathy.

Brain Science Insight: The process of resolving a conflict helps strengthen the connections between the **amygdala** and the **prefrontal cortex**. This is essential for emotional regulation. Think of each sibling fight as a mini brain workout—they're lifting emotional weights. And just like with physical workouts, it takes repetition to build strength. The more they practice handling conflicts (with your guidance), the stronger their emotional regulation becomes.

Why It's Not All Bad (But It Still Feels That Way)

Here's the thing: sibling rivalry feels incredibly personal to you, the parent, because it often happens in the middle of dinner, during family movie night, or right after you've told them for the 10th time that "we don't hit in this house." But while it feels chaotic, it's actually a **normal part of brain development**.

- **Young kids** are learning how to manage their big feelings, and that means pushing boundaries (and each other).

- **Older kids** are testing their place in the world and figuring out how to handle frustrations and perceived injustices.

- **Teens** are a whole other level, with their developing prefrontal cortexes, hormonal shifts, and emotional chaos, but their teasing and instigating are often ways of asserting their own growing independence.

When It's More Than Normal

That said, there are times when sibling rivalry can escalate to a point where intervention is needed. If the fights become excessively physical, or one child seems to be consistently victimized, it's important to step in more directly. This might mean family discussions about respect, clearer boundaries, or, in some cases, speaking to a professional to help the kids navigate their emotions in a healthier way.

The End Goal: Siblings Who (Sometimes) Get Along

At the end of the day, my goal isn't to raise kids who never fight (because that's just not realistic). My goal is to help them develop the emotional tools to handle conflict in a way that doesn't involve head pats, shoves, or dramatic accusations of unfairness. And sure, there are days when I feel like a broken record, repeating the same phrases over and over again: "Use your words," "Take a deep breath," "Respect goes both ways." But every once in a while, I catch a glimpse of progress—a moment when they solve a problem on their own, take a breath instead of throwing a punch, or, miracle of miracles, actually help each other.

And on those days, I remind myself that brain development is a slow process. It's messy, chaotic, and full of learning curves. But with a little patience, a lot of humour, and some solid brain science, I'm confident that one day, these squabbling siblings will grow into adults who can navigate conflict without needing a referee.

Chapter 6

Brain Food: Feeding Hungry Minds Without Losing Yours

If there's one thing I've learned after raising three kids, it's that *feeding them* feels like running a 24/7 restaurant, only with much more whining and zero tips. Between picky eaters, sudden growth spurts, and their insatiable ability to snack, feeding kids is no small feat. Add to that the pressure to make sure they're eating brain-boosting foods (you know, the ones you read about in that one article while waiting for your coffee), and suddenly, it feels like meal planning should come with a PhD in nutrition.

Here's the thing: what we feed our kids directly impacts their brain development. We're not just feeding their bodies; we're feeding their minds, too. But that doesn't mean you have to turn your kitchen into a quinoa-and-kale-only zone. There are ways to fuel their brains without losing your sanity or waging war over vegetables every night. So, let's dive into the world of brain food, how it affects your kids, and of course, a few mom hacks to make sure everyone eats something that didn't come from a box.

Why Brain Food Matters (Without Getting Too Sciencey)

Before we get into the nitty-gritty of what to feed these little humans, let's talk about why it even matters. Our brains are energy-hungry organs. In fact, the brain uses around 20% of the body's total energy, which means it needs a steady supply of good nutrients to function at its best—especially for kids whose brains are developing at lightning speed.

You know those days when your kid is bouncing off the walls like a sugar-powered pinball? That's because their brains, particularly the **prefrontal cortex** (responsible for decision-making and self-control), are incredibly sensitive to what they eat. Blood sugar spikes from sugary snacks make them feel like superheroes for 10 minutes before they crash—and take the rest of the family down with them.

But the good news is, the right foods can help keep their energy levels stable, support cognitive development, and (dare I say) even improve their mood. And trust me, anything that helps with mood improvement is worth its weight in gold.

Mom Hack 1: The Sneaky Brain Boosters

Okay, let's be real. If I told my six-year-old that he was getting "omega-3-rich salmon" for dinner to boost his brain function, he'd look at me like I had two heads and then demand macaroni and cheese.

So instead of getting into the details, I've learned to sneak brain-boosting foods into meals in ways they don't even notice. I call it my covert nutrition mission.

The Secret Ingredient Switcheroo:

- **Smoothies**: These are your new best friend. I toss in things like spinach, chia seeds, or flaxseeds (hello, omega-3s!) into their fruit smoothies, and they never know. All they taste is the banana and strawberries, but their brains are getting the good stuff.

- **Eggs with a Twist**: Eggs are great for brain development because they're packed with choline, which helps with memory. My six-year-old won't eat eggs unless they look like scrambled clouds, so I mix them with some finely grated veggies like carrots or spinach, and voilà—veggie-packed eggs that still look like his idea of acceptable food.

Mom Hack 2: Negotiating the Non-Negotiables

I have one kid who refuses to touch anything green (yes, I see you, 6-year-old), another who thinks ketchup is a vegetable (hello, 9-year-old), and a teenager who subsists on a diet of sarcasm and pastries. So, getting them to eat a balanced diet requires negotiation skills that would put a United Nations diplomat to shame.

The 80/20 Rule:

Here's the deal: I aim for 80% healthy and 20% whatever keeps the peace. This means that if my teenager insists on having her slice of cake as a snack, I'll throw in some nuts or a slice of avocado toast on the side. The key is to focus on balance rather than perfection. We can't win every battle, but we can make small wins count.

Why Sugar Makes Your Kids Act Like Gremlins

Let's talk about sugar for a second. Every parent has seen the immediate aftermath of a sugar binge—the wild-eyed, hyperactive burst of energy followed by the inevitable crash that leaves everyone cranky and exhausted. It's like watching a tiny human turn into a gremlin before your very eyes.

Brain Science Insight: Sugar causes a quick spike in blood sugar levels, leading to an equally quick crash. When the sugar high hits, their **dopamine** levels (the feel-good hormone) go through the roof, making them feel invincible. But when it wears off, their energy drops, and they're left feeling irritable, tired, and ready to meltdown over the slightest inconvenience—like how someone *dared* to look at them during snack time.

Mom Hack (How to Handle Sugar Without Losing Your Mind):

I don't ban sugar completely because that just makes it more appealing (forbidden fruit and all that). Instead, I try to pair sugary treats with protein or fiber to help balance out the blood sugar spike. For example, if they're having a cookie, I'll serve it with a handful of almonds or a slice of cheese. It slows down the sugar absorption and prevents the crash-and-burn scenario.

Mom Hack 3: Let Them Make Choices (But Guide Them)

I've found that giving my kids some autonomy over what they eat makes them more likely to choose healthier options. But of course, I don't just open the pantry and say, "Have at it." Instead, I give them **guided choices**: "Do you want an apple or a banana with your sandwich?" or "Would you like carrots or cucumbers with your humus?"

The Power of Choice:

The simple act of letting them choose makes them feel more in control, and their brain loves that. It engages their **prefrontal cortex**, helping them learn decision-making and impulse control. Plus, when they feel like they're in charge, they're more likely to eat what's offered instead of rejecting it on principle.

Mom Hack 4: Make It Fun (Even If You're Exhausted)

I'm not saying every meal has to look like it was prepared by Pinterest moms with endless patience, but making food fun does help. When food looks appealing, kids are more likely to try it—especially if you get them involved in the process. I've found that when my kids help prepare meals, they're more excited to eat them, even if it's just cutting up fruit or sprinkling cheese on a dish.

Food as Art:

- **Funny Faces**: Turn lunch into an art project. Use veggie sticks, fruits, or cheese to create funny faces on their plate. Somehow, a cucumber nose and carrot hair make everything taste better.

- **DIY Tacos**: I set up a taco bar once a week where the kids can choose their own toppings. They love the sense of control, and I love that they end up eating things like black beans and avocado without complaint.

Final Thoughts: Feeding Their Brains Without Losing Yours

Let's be real - parenting in the 21st century isn't just about keeping our kids fed, it's about doing it in a world where unhealthy food is more accessible than ever. Between fast food delivery apps, snack aisles that stretch for miles, and the endless stream of sugar-filled treats marketed to kids, it's no wonder we sometimes feel like we're fighting an uphill battle. We're supposed to be feeding their brains and keeping them healthy, but also surviving the daily chaos of life, where a meal from Swiggy or Zomato feels like the most achievable solution on some days.

So, if you've ever had to order a pizza because your day spiralled out of control, or if your kids have consumed more than their fair share of instant noodles, trust me—you're not alone. As much as I'd love to say that every meal in our house is a perfectly balanced, brain-boosting, Pinterest-worthy creation, the reality is that some days it's just about getting through dinner without anyone crying (including me).

The Struggle is Real (and It's Okay to Take Shortcuts)

We live in a fast-paced world, and sometimes the fastest solution wins. And that's okay! Feeding kids isn't about hitting perfection every time; it's about finding a balance that works for your family. Yes, brain food is important, but so is your mental health. If that means frozen chicken nuggets one night and a home-cooked veggie-packed meal the next, you're doing great.

Mindful Eating in the Modern World

What I've learned is that we can still be mindful about what we feed our kids without feeling guilty for the shortcuts. It's not about avoiding takeout forever; it's about making small, sustainable choices that add up over time. The key is awareness. On busy days, fast food might be the easiest option, but when we have the time (and energy), we can balance it with meals that nourish their growing brains.

Mom Hack (Embrace the Imperfection): If dinner ends up being fast food or something less than ideal, I let it go and move on. What matters is that over time, I'm offering healthy, brain-boosting options. One less-than-perfect meal won't undo all the good. If my kids get the nutrients, they need most of the time, I consider that a win. Plus, when I'm not beating myself up over every meal, I can enjoy the moments when they do eat that avocado toast or spinach smoothie without a fight.

Why Empathy Matters (for Yourself and Your Kids)

Parenting is hard. Feeding kids, with all their quirks, preferences, and growth spurts, is even harder. We live in a world of convenience, where it feels like we're constantly bombarded by quick, easy (but not always healthy) food options. Add in the stress of work, school, extracurriculars, and, well, life in general, and it's no wonder we're reaching for those delivery apps. It's important to cut yourself some slack and recognize that you're doing your best.

Being empathetic toward ourselves is just as important as showing empathy to our kids. They're still learning about food, their bodies, and their brains. The battles over broccoli or the meltdown over not getting dessert are just as frustrating for them as they are for us. By understanding that we're all navigating this food journey together, we can create a more mindful, compassionate environment for both ourselves and our children.

Mom Hack (Mindfulness in Small Doses): Instead of trying to overhaul everything at once, I focus on small changes. If we've had a fast-food dinner, I might serve fruit with breakfast the next day. If snacks have been too sugary lately, I swap in some nuts or cheese. These little adjustments help create a healthier overall balance without feeling overwhelming or impossible.

Mindful Choices, Not Perfect Choices

At the end of the day, it's not about making the *perfect* choices—it's about making **mindful** ones. Can we always prepare a brain-boosting meal from scratch? Of course not. But we can be aware of what we're feeding our kids and why it matters. We can try to offer them foods that help their brains grow and develop, while also knowing that life happens, and sometimes, the most important thing is just getting everyone fed before bedtime.

In this fast-food world, being mindful doesn't mean being perfect. It means taking a moment to recognize that while food fuels their bodies and brains, it's also an opportunity to bond, to teach them about balance, and to show them that healthy choices are part of life—not all of it.

So yes, there will be days when you resort to delivery. There will be moments when cereal is dinner (I've been there). But as long as we're mindful of the bigger picture—of nourishing their growing brains, balancing indulgence with nutrition, and doing the best we can with what we've got—we're already winning.

And when all else fails? There's always that trusty smoothie.

Chapter 7
The Power of Play

Why Their Brain Needs It More Than You Think

If I had a dollar for every time my kids have said, "Can I just play for five more minutes?" I'd be lounging on a tropical beach instead of negotiating over Legos and video game time. Playtime, in all its chaotic, noisy glory, seems like the universal request of children everywhere. My two boys—who attend the Montessori school where play is not only encouraged but woven into their daily learning—seem to think playtime is a human right. And honestly? They're not wrong.

Meanwhile, my teenage daughter, who began her early childhood days in a Montessori environment, looks at me like I'm speaking another language when I suggest she "go play outside." Apparently, once they hit their teens, "play" transforms into "texting" or "eye-rolling marathons," but that's another chapter for another day.

Here's the thing: play is not just about keeping kids entertained or distracted so you can finish your coffee (though that's definitely a perk). Play is how children learn, grow, and develop the critical skills they'll need for the rest of their lives. And, as a Montessori mom, I've seen firsthand how powerful and brain-boosting play can be when it's done right.

The Brain Science Behind Play: Why It's Serious Business

First, let's bust the myth that play is "just" play. The truth is, play is serious business for your child's brain. In fact, it's one of the most important ways they learn. Play stimulates the development of key areas in the brain, especially the **prefrontal cortex**, which is responsible for decision-making, problem-solving, and regulating emotions. So while it may look like they're just stacking blocks or pretending to be superheroes, their brain is working hard to make sense of the world, build connections, and strengthen critical cognitive skills.

In a Montessori environment—like the one my boys are in—play is seamlessly integrated into their learning. Montessori views play as "work," and trust me, when you see a six-year-old completely absorbed in figuring out how to build a tower that won't fall over, you'll realize just how right they are.

Montessori and Play: The Perfect Brain-Boosting Combo

Let me tell you, there's nothing like watching your kids work (and play) in a Montessori classroom. My boys, who are in the elementary years at their Montessori school, thrive in an environment where they can follow their interests, learn at their own pace, and—this is the best part—do all of this while engaging in play-based activities. Montessori is all about hands-on, sensory-rich experiences that make learning feel natural. It's not just sitting at a desk all day (not that they would tolerate that anyway).

In Montessori, play isn't random; it's purposeful. Activities like building with blocks, pouring water between containers, or sorting objects by colour and size help kids develop **executive function** skills, which are crucial for planning, organizing, and staying focused. These are all things the prefrontal cortex is responsible for, and let's face it, anything that helps kids develop focus is a gift from the parenting gods.

Real-Life Example: My six-year-old spent an entire afternoon building an elaborate "city" out of wooden blocks. He was so absorbed in his task that I could have probably set off fireworks next to him, and he wouldn't have flinched. He explained to me, in great detail, how the bridges had to be just the right height for the toy cars to pass under. Sure, it looked like he was "just playing," but his brain was busy developing spatial reasoning, problem-solving, and concentration skills. And I got an hour of peace. A win-win.

Mom Hack: Playtime as a Brain Workout

Instead of thinking of play as a way to kill time before dinner (though that's valid), think of it as a brain workout. Every time your child engages in free play—whether it's building a fort out of couch cushions or pretending to be a chef making mud pies—they're exercising their **prefrontal cortex**. This helps them develop critical life skills like **impulse control**, **emotional regulation**, and **problem-solving**. In other words, play helps your child learn how to be a functioning human.

So, when my 9-year-old is deep in a world of imaginary battles with action figures, I remind myself (through clenched teeth, as I step on a stray toy) that his brain is doing the mental equivalent of CrossFit.

Mom Hack (Balancing Screen Time with Real Play): While it's tempting to hand over the tablet when you need a break (guilty!), I've found that setting designated "screen-free play times" helps keep things balanced. We have a rule where afternoons after school are for physical or imaginative play—whether it's outside, with Legos, or art projects. This gives their brains a chance to decompress, explore, and develop creative thinking without the overstimulation of screens.

Real-Life Example: Last week, I watched my boys turn the living room into a "campground" complete with a makeshift tent, "campfire," and rock collections. They spent hours problem-solving how to construct the perfect campsite (without toppling the lamp), and it took every ounce of my patience not to intervene when things collapsed. But here's the thing—they figured it out on their own. Their brains worked overtime, and when they finally nailed it, they beamed with pride. (I beamed with relief that no one broke anything valuable.)

The Teenage Twist: Play Evolves

Now, let's talk about play when it comes to my teenage daughter. When she was younger and in her Montessori days, she thrived in that environment where play was learning. She was always the one building elaborate structures, working on puzzles, and getting lost in pretend play. But as she hit her teen years, play evolved into something more "mature" (according to her, at least). Now, play is more about socializing, texting friends, and occasionally rolling her eyes when I suggest family board game night.

Here's where brain science comes in: the **prefrontal cortex** is still developing in teens, and while play might look different for them, it's still essential. For my daughter, play looks more like creative hobbies—drawing, baking, or writing stories—and it's just as important for her brain as it was when she was younger. These activities still engage her **executive function** skills, just in more subtle ways.

Mom Hack (Getting Teens to "Play"): I've found that giving her space to engage in her own version of play—whether it's art projects or baking—is the key to keeping her creative brain active. While she's no longer stacking blocks or building forts, she's still doing activities that require problem-solving and creativity, even if it's disguised as making elaborate TikTok videos. She is currently working on creating a promotional video of my school for social media!

The Science of Free Play vs. Structured Play

Let's talk about the balance between **free play** and **structured play**. Both are important, but free play—the kind where your kids run wild with their imaginations and make up their own rules—has a special place in brain development. It helps kids practice decision-making, social skills, and conflict resolution, especially when they're playing with siblings (and yes, that often leads to fights, but stay with me).

In a Montessori setting, there's a beautiful blend of structured activities with free play. For example, my boys might work with a

Montessori "material" like the Pink Tower, carefully stacking the blocks in order, and then move into free play where they build an entire city with those same blocks. Both types of play help develop their brains, but in different ways.

Mom Hack: Let Them Be Bored

This one's hard, I know. We live in a world where there's always something to entertain our kids, whether it's a screen, a toy, or an activity we've planned for them. But boredom is actually a powerful tool for brain development. When kids are bored, their brains kick into gear, and they start finding creative ways to entertain themselves. It's during these moments that their **prefrontal cortex** gets a workout, as they're forced to come up with new ideas, solve problems, and use their imaginations.

Real-Life Example: One Saturday afternoon, when I was knee-deep in laundry, my boys came to me with the dreaded phrase, "We're bored." Instead of offering suggestions, I said, "Well, you guys are smart, figure it out." After some grumbling, they wandered off, and 20 minutes later, I found them working with paints, creating their own versions of a messy Picasso! No doubt, I had to clear the mess up later, but, sometimes, boredom is the best gift we can give them.

Why Play Isn't Just for Kids (Parents Need It Too)

Here's a secret: play isn't just for the kids. We need it, too. As parents, we're so wrapped up in keeping the household running, managing work, and trying to keep everyone alive, that we forget how important play is for our own well-being. Play helps reduce stress, boosts creativity, and gives our overworked adult brains a much-needed break.

Mom Hack (Play with Your Kids, Even if It's Silly): I know, I know—playing the 47th round of "guess what animal I am" might not be your idea of fun. But when I take a few minutes to get down on their level and engage in their world, not only does it strengthen our bond, but I also get to let go of the day's stresses. Plus, nothing beats the look on their faces when you're willing to be silly with them, even if it means pretending to be a pirate or crawling through a blanket fort. Play isn't just a tool for them to grow—it's a reminder for us to lighten up and connect on their level. It's not always about *what* you play, but that you're there, joining in.

Final Thoughts: The Power of Play

As a mom with three kids at different stages of life—from my 6-year-old, who lives for building block towers, to my 9-year-old, who's always in search of an imaginary adventure, to my 16-year-old, whose version of play is crafting the perfect TikTok or whipping up a batch of cupcakes—play looks different for each of them. But it's all equally important.

In a world where schedules are packed, and screens are everywhere, making time for real, imaginative, brain-building play isn't just a luxury—it's essential. Play nurtures their growing brains, teaches them vital life skills, and reminds them (and us) that learning happens in the most unexpected and joyful ways.

Whether it's structured Montessori "work" or free-spirited creative play, what may seem like just another game to them is actually an investment in their cognitive and emotional growth. And if we can join in from time to time, laugh a little more, and embrace the chaos, we'll be growing right along with them.

So the next time your kids are deep in their own imaginative worlds—or pestering you to join them—remember that play is their brain's playground. And hey, it's good for your brain, too.

Chapter 8

Raising Critical Thinkers: Why 'Because I Said So' Doesn't Work Anymore

Ah, the golden phrase of parenting: "Because I said so." If only it worked past the toddler years! There's something beautifully simple about being able to end a debate with those four words. But as any parent of a slightly older child knows, this magical phrase starts to lose its power right around the time they figure out they have their own thoughts—and, let's be honest, a *lot* of opinions.

Now, I'm parenting three critical thinkers: a 16-year-old who's basically a walking argument, a 9-year-old who has questions about every rule I make, and a 6-year-old who's mastered the art of "Why?" at a level that rivals the most curious philosophers. Somewhere along the way, "because I said so" transformed from a satisfying end to an argument into a trigger for a whole new one.

And that's not necessarily a bad thing. Brain science shows us that the more questions they ask, the better their brains develop. Great! Except when I'm trying to explain why the Lego bricks *absolutely* need to be cleaned up before bed and not later, while my 9-year-old is launching into a debate about creative freedom.

Let's dive into why raising critical thinkers is so important, what's going on in their growing brains, and how we can survive the constant "why?" bombardment while encouraging their budding intellectual skills.

Why 'Because I Said So' No Longer Works (and Why That's a Good Thing)

It turns out, when your kids start questioning your every move, it's a sign their **prefrontal cortex** is kicking into high gear. This part of the brain, responsible for reasoning, problem-solving, and decision-making, is developing at full speed during childhood and adolescence. So, when my 9-year-old wants to know why he can't stay up until 11 p.m. to finish building his spaceship, his brain is practicing critical thinking. As frustrating as the endless questions are, they're helping him make sense of the world - and figure out how to work within (and sometimes against) the boundaries we set as parents.

For my 16-year-old, questioning authority (me) is practically a hobby. Teens are notorious for pushing back because their **prefrontal cortex** is undergoing major reconstruction. They're not just testing the limits - they're actively trying to develop independence and practice decision-making, which is both impressive and exhausting. There are moments when I find myself in a full-on debate about why screen time limits exist, and I'll admit, sometimes her arguments are pretty compelling.

Brain Science Insight: The development of the **prefrontal cortex** takes years—like, into their mid-20s years - so this questioning phase is far from over. But it's essential for building the kind of brain that can think critically, solve problems, and ultimately, make sound decisions. So, while it's tempting to drop a quick "because I said so," it's more productive (and brain-boosting) to engage in the conversation, even if it means enduring a few eye rolls.

Mom Hack: The Art of Negotiation (with a 9-Year-Old Lawyer)

It's easy to get sucked into endless negotiations with kids, especially when they're armed with a fresh set of reasoning skills. My 9-year-old, in particular, could probably win a small court case with his ability to argue his way out of chores. His go-to phrase is, "But what if..." and suddenly I'm down a rabbit hole where everything is hypothetical, and nothing is certain.

Mom Hack (Avoid the Debate Loop): Instead of getting trapped in negotiations, I've learned to redirect his questions. When he asks, "But what if I don't go to sleep early tonight?" I calmly ask, "What do you think would happen?" This throws the ball back in his court and forces him to think through the consequences. Often, he realizes that his "what ifs" lead back to the same conclusion I had in the first place: Yes, I need to get my sleep to get to school in the morning bright and ready. Boom - problem solved without a 30-minute debate.

Teaching the 6-Year-Old: The Why Phase is a Brain Workout

Ah, the 6-year-old and the relentless "why" phase. There are days when I think he's trying to break a world record for the most questions asked before lunch. And while it's tempting to answer with "because I said so" just to end the conversation, I know that his constant questioning is actually his brain's way of figuring out how the world works.

At this age, his brain is buzzing with curiosity, and his **prefrontal cortex** is just beginning to develop its reasoning skills. The **amygdala** (emotional brain) still holds a lot of sway, which means he's emotionally invested in finding out *why* things happen the way they do. Whether it's "Why is the sky blue?" or "Why can't I have cookies for breakfast?", every question helps build the neural connections that will support higher-level thinking down the road.

Mom Hack (Answer the Important Whys, Sidestep the Rest): I've learned that I don't have to answer every single "why" question in depth. Some questions deserve thoughtful answers, especially when they're about the world or how things work. But when we're on question #45 about why we can't adopt a pet dragon, I sidestep with humor: "Because dragons are on vacation this week, sweetie." That buys me a few minutes of peace before the next "why" shows up.

My 6-year-old recently asked me, "Why can't I eat cookies for every meal?" Instead of diving into a full nutritional lesson, I went with, "Well, if you ate only cookies, your brain wouldn't get the superpowers it needs to grow strong and smart." He liked the idea of his brain having superpowers, and just like that, we avoided a sugar-filled meal plan.

The Teen Brain: Independence and the Constant Pushback

Parenting a teen is like being part of a long-running debate club, except I'm not sure I signed up for it. My 16-year-old is in that beautiful phase where she questions every rule I make - not because she's rebellious (okay, maybe a little), but because her brain is wired to seek independence. The teenage **prefrontal cortex** is a work-in-progress, and it's trying to figure out how to manage the flood of emotions from the **amygdala**, while also developing logical decision-making skills.

This is why teens seem to push back on *everything*. They're testing boundaries, flexing their independence, and practicing the decision-making skills they'll need as adults. The constant "But why can't I…?" isn't just an attempt to be difficult - it's their way of learning how to navigate the adult world.

Mom Hack (Help Them Practice Decision-Making): When my teen pushes back, instead of immediately shutting her down, I let her practice her reasoning skills. I ask, "Why do you think this rule is in place?" or "What would you do if you were the parent?" Often, this leads to a more meaningful conversation about responsibility, consequences, and independence - without turning into a full-on argument.

Real-Life Example: My daughter recently challenged the handing over the phone at night rule, arguing that it "wasn't a big deal." Instead of saying "because I said so," I asked her to explain why she felt that way. After some back-and-forth, we agreed that while her phone could be important, night was a time rest. She didn't love it, but by the end, she understood the reasoning—and we avoided the typical teenage eye-roll fest.

Encouraging Critical Thinking Without Losing Your Mind

Here's the key to raising critical thinkers: it's about guiding their questions rather than shutting them down. I try to engage their brains, even when I'm exhausted from explaining why no, we can't have a pet dragon. The more I help them work through their questions, the more confident they become in their ability to solve problems on their own. Plus, it saves me from having to answer "why" 200 times a day.

And yes, there are moments when I'll resort to "because I said so" because it's bedtime, and we all need sleep. But overall, fostering critical thinking is one of the best gifts we can give our kids—it helps them build a brain that's ready for life's challenges (and, let's be honest, prepares them for those future debates where they *might* just have a point).

So, the next time your child asks "why," take a deep breath and remind yourself that you're raising a critical thinker - and that their questions, though endless, are building the brain power they'll need for the rest of their lives.

Chapter 9
Sleep, Screens, and Stress: How to Keep Their Brains Healthy in a Hyper-Stimulated World

If you asked me to name the three things that wreak havoc on my kids' behaviour, I'd have to say lack of sleep, too much screen time, and—you guessed it—stress. Unfortunately, in today's world, these three often go hand-in-hand, like a parenting trifecta of chaos. Between endless digital distractions, the pressure of school and activities, and their ever-changing sleep patterns, I feel like I'm constantly playing whack-a-mole with their mood swings.

Sleep deprivation turns my normally sweet 6-year-old into a tiny dictator, my 9-year-old into a puddle of irrationality, and my 16-year-old into a sarcastic sleep-deprived teenager (okay, that one might just be normal). Add too much screen time to the mix, and we've got a recipe for overstimulation, meltdowns, and eye rolls that could power a small city.

But here's the kicker: all of this—the sleep, the screens, the stress—is not just affecting their behaviour in the moment. It's also affecting their **brain development**, especially when it comes to emotional regulation, focus, and cognitive growth. So how do we keep their brains healthy in a world that seems determined to overstimulate them? Let's dive into the brain science behind it all, and, of course, some tried-and-tested mom hacks to keep the chaos at bay.

Why Sleep Is a Brain's Best Friend
(Why It's So Hard to Get Enough)

Let's start with the one thing every parent obsesses over: sleep. When my kids are well-rested, they're (mostly) rational, calm, and able to manage their emotions. When they're sleep-deprived? It's like living with miniature, emotional tornadoes. And honestly, I'm no better without sleep, but that's a different chapter.

The brain needs sleep to function properly, especially for kids. During sleep, their brains go through a process called **synaptic pruning**, which helps remove unnecessary connections and strengthen important ones. It's like a nightly brain clean-up session, and without it, their ability to focus, learn, and regulate emotions takes a hit.

Brain Science Insight: Sleep is critical for the development of the **prefrontal cortex**, the part of the brain responsible for decision-making, impulse control, and problem-solving. Without enough sleep, this part of the brain doesn't work at full capacity, which explains why tired kids are more impulsive, emotional, and prone to meltdowns.

Mom Hack (Creating a Sleep Routine Without Losing Your Mind):

I've learned that consistency is key when it comes to bedtime routines. With my 6-year-old, it's all about predictable steps: bath, book, bed. For my 9-year-old, we've added a calming activity (usually reading or quiet play) about 30 minutes before bed to help his brain wind down. And for my 16-year-old? Well, I've had to get creative. We have a no-phones-in-the-bedroom rule (which she loves to hate), but it helps her brain disconnect from the digital world before sleep.

Screens: The Modern-Day Brain Drain

Ah, screens. Whether it's the TV, the tablet, or the phone, screens are like magnets for my kids' attention—and a guaranteed way to turn them into zombies if left unchecked. Don't get me wrong, I'm no screen-time purist. Sometimes, handing over the tablet is the only way I get a moment of peace. But I've noticed a direct correlation between excessive screen time and behaviour shifts, especially when it comes to focus, mood, and sleep.

Here's why - **Screens stimulate the brain's reward system** by releasing **dopamine**, the feel-good chemical that makes them want to keep playing, watching, or scrolling. The problem is, the more dopamine they get from screens, the more their brains crave it, making it harder for them to stay engaged with non-digital activities (like, you know, real life).

Brain Science Insight: Too much screen time, especially before bed, messes with the brain's production of **melatonin**, the hormone responsible for regulating sleep. This is why kids who've been glued to a screen before bed often struggle to fall asleep, and when they do sleep, it's not as restful. It's like their brain is stuck in "on" mode, even when their body is exhausted.

Mom Hack (Setting Screen Limits Without Revolt): In our house, we have a screen time "curfew." All screens go off at least an hour before bedtime. It wasn't easy at first—there were protests, negotiations, and eye rolls (mostly from the teenager)—but over time, it's become part of the routine. For the younger two, I offer alternatives like drawing, reading, or even board games before bed. For my teen, we've compromised with some "wind down" time, where she listens to music or podcasts (no screens) before lights out.

Managing Stress: When Life Overloads Their Brains

Let's talk about stress. We think of it as an adult problem, but kids experience it too, often in ways we don't even notice. Between school pressures, social dynamics, and the constant stimulation of the modern world, their little brains are often on overload.

When kids experience stress, their **amygdala** (the emotional center of the brain) goes into overdrive. This triggers the **fight-or-flight** response, making it harder for the **prefrontal cortex** to do its job—things like problem-solving, impulse control, and emotional regulation. The result? Meltdowns, mood swings, and, occasionally, a 6-year-old lying on the floor dramatically refusing to put on socks.

Brain Science Insight: Chronic stress impacts brain development, especially in kids, by overloading the **hypothalamus-pituitary-adrenal (HPA) axis**, which regulates the body's response to stress. Over time, this can affect memory, learning, and emotional resilience, which is why it's so important to help kids manage stress in healthy ways.

Mom Hack (Building Stress-Busting Routines): We've introduced some "brain calming" routines in our house to help the kids (and let's be honest, me) manage stress. Simple things like deep breathing exercises, guided meditation for kids, or even just talking through their worries can make a huge difference. For my younger two, we sometimes do "worry journaling," where they draw or write about what's bothering them. For my teen, it's about creating space for her to vent without judgment, then helping her brainstorm ways to manage the stress.

Mom Hack: Modelling Healthy Habits (Yes, It Matters)

Here's the part that's not always easy to hear: our kids are watching us. If I'm staying up late, glued to my phone, or letting stress rule my day, they notice. Their brains are wired to imitate what they see, especially from us. So, if I want them to develop healthy sleep, screen, and stress management habits, I need to model them too (no pressure, right?).

Real-Life Example: I've started joining my kids during their "wind down" time before bed. We all do a few minutes of deep breathing, stretch, or read quietly together. Not only does it help them calm down, but it forces me to put my phone away and relax, too. And on nights when I'm tempted to check email or scroll through social media before bed, I remind myself that my brain needs a break just as much as theirs.

Final Thoughts: Finding Balance in a Hyper-Stimulated World

Keeping kids' brains healthy in a world full of screens, stress, and sleep challenges can feel like juggling flaming swords while riding a unicycle. But here's the good news: it's not about perfection, it's about balance. It's okay if they have the occasional late-night movie marathon or a stressful day at school. What matters is helping them develop the tools to manage it all in healthy ways—whether that's sticking to a bedtime routine, setting screen limits, or teaching them how to navigate stress.

And as parents, we're not just guiding them through this—we're navigating it ourselves. So be kind to yourself when the bedtime battle takes longer than expected or when screen time creeps in a little more than planned. As long as we're mindful of the balance, we're doing exactly what their growing brains need.

Chapter 10
The Parent Brain: How to Be the Calm in the Chaos (Even When Your Kids Aren't)

If there's one thing I've learned after raising three kids, it's that the whole "keep calm and carry on" mantra is easier said than done. With a 16-year-old who likes to debate everything from curfews to the meaning of life, a 9-year-old who can throw a tantrum worthy of an Olympic medal over misplaced Lego bricks, and a 6-year-old who turns bedtime into a Broadway production, staying calm sometimes feels like an impossible dream. But here's the kicker: **our brains** are the key to keeping the chaos under control.

Parenting is all about managing chaos, but what no one tells you is that half the battle is managing your own brain in the process. When my kids are in full meltdown mode or stirring up sibling drama for the tenth time that day, I feel like a referee who's just trying to stay in the game. And yet, science tells us that the calmer **we** stay, the more likely we are to calm *them* down.

The reality is, our children's developing brains are still figuring out how to manage emotions, impulses, and stress. And guess whose brain is responsible for showing them how? Yep, it's ours—the parent brain.

So, let's dive into the science of how staying calm in the chaos can help regulate not just their brains, but ours, too. Plus, we'll cover some mom-tested hacks to avoid losing it when the Legos hit the fan.

Your Brain on Parenting: Why Calm is Contagious

When kids lose control, their **amygdala**—the part of the brain responsible for emotional responses—takes over. This is why tantrums, meltdowns, and irrational outbursts happen. And when they're in this emotional state, they're not thinking logically (trust me, there's no point in reasoning with a six-year-old mid-meltdown about why they can't have ice cream for breakfast). Their **prefrontal cortex**—the part of the brain responsible for self-regulation and decision-making—is offline in these moments.

But here's the good news: **our calmness** can actually help bring their brain back online. When we stay calm in the face of their emotional outbursts, we model emotional regulation, and through a process called **co-regulation**, their brain begins to mirror ours. In other words, our calm is contagious.

Brain Science Insight: When you stay calm, you're essentially lending your child's brain your prefrontal cortex while theirs is temporarily out of order. This helps them move from an emotional state back to a more logical, regulated one. But if we lose our cool, their brain picks up on our stress, and their **amygdala** stays in overdrive, escalating the situation.

Mom Hack (Breathe First, React Later): One trick I've learned is to take a deep breath (or five) before responding to whatever chaos is unfolding. I'm not always great at it, especially when the boys are going at it, but those few seconds of pause help me get my own emotions in check before I react. And let's be honest, it's also a quick way to stop myself from saying something I'll regret later.

Why Your Calmness is the Best Discipline Tool

Let's be clear: discipline is necessary. But what I've realized (through much trial and error) is that when I discipline from a place of anger or frustration, it usually backfires. My kids don't learn anything except that Mom's mad, which is exactly what the **amygdala** in their brain focuses on—my emotional state, not their behaviour.

Brain Science Insight: The goal of discipline is to teach, not punish. When we stay calm during discipline, we engage their prefrontal cortex, helping them learn from their mistakes and make better choices next time. On the flip side, yelling or reacting out of frustration keeps their brain in **fight-or-flight mode**, preventing them from actually processing what we're trying to teach them.

Mom Hack (The Calm Down Corner): In our house, we have a "calm down corner." It's not a timeout in the traditional sense, but a quiet space with soft pillows, books, and some sensory items like stress balls. When one of my kids is on the verge of losing it (or has already lost it), I'll calmly suggest they spend a few minutes in the calm down corner to reset. Sometimes, I even go with them, because let's face it—I could use a timeout, too.

The Power of Empathy (Even When You're Over It)

If I had to pick one thing that's made the biggest difference in keeping my cool as a parent, it's empathy. When my kids are acting out, I remind myself that their brains are still developing, and sometimes, they simply don't have the tools to manage their big emotions. Instead of reacting with frustration, I try to put myself in their shoes.

Empathy as a Brain Hack: When I respond to their behavior with empathy—acknowledging their feelings without giving in to their demands—it helps calm their **amygdala** and engages their prefrontal cortex. They feel heard, which reduces the emotional intensity of the situation, and they're more likely to cooperate.

How to Reset Your Own Brain When the Chaos Hits

Let's be real: there are days when keeping calm feels impossible. Between juggling work, the kids, and a thousand other things, my **stress levels** can spike just as easily as theirs. And when that happens, my **amygdala** takes over, too, and I end up snapping, yelling, or feeling totally overwhelmed. The truth is, our brains need regulation just as much as our kids' brains do. And when we're stressed or emotionally drained, it's harder to be the calm, rational parent we want to be.

So, how do we reset our own brains when the chaos hits, and we feel like we're about to lose it? It starts with recognizing that **we** need self-care and regulation, just as much as our kids do.

Mom Hack: Build Your Own Calm-Down Routine

Let's face it, we're not superhuman (though some days it feels like we have to be). To stay calm in the face of chaos, we need our own strategies to hit the reset button. For me, that means finding small pockets of peace throughout the day—whether it's a 5-minute coffee break, a quick walk around the block, or sneaking into the bathroom just for a moment of silence (yep, it's come to that).

When I feel my stress rising, I use a quick **mindfulness technique** called "box breathing." It's simple: inhale for four counts, hold for four counts, exhale for four counts, hold again, and repeat. This helps regulate my **nervous system**, bringing me out of fight-or-flight mode and back into my logical brain. It's amazing how a few deep breaths can stop me from reacting in ways I'll regret later.

Mom Hack: The Magic of the 'Pause' Button

When your kids are melting down and your stress levels are skyrocketing, the instinct to react immediately is strong. But one of the best brain-based strategies I've learned is to hit the mental "pause" button. Pausing gives your brain time to catch up with your emotions, allowing you to respond calmly instead of reacting impulsively.

Brain Science Insight: When you pause before responding, you engage your **prefrontal cortex**, the part of the brain responsible for thinking and reasoning. This helps you avoid reacting out of frustration (which is driven by the **amygdala**) and instead choose a more thoughtful response.

Mom Hack: Model Apology and Repair

Let's be real—there are going to be moments when we lose our cool. We're human, after all. But here's the thing: those moments don't have to derail the whole day. One of the most powerful things we can do as parents is model how to apologize and repair after we've lost our temper. This shows our kids that even grown-ups make mistakes, and it teaches them the importance of taking responsibility for their actions.

Brain Science Insight: When we model apology and repair, we activate our kids' **mirror neurons**, the part of the brain that helps them learn by observing others. By showing them how to handle mistakes with grace, we're teaching them valuable emotional regulation and problem-solving skills.

A few days ago, I snapped at my 9-year-old for something minor—I was tired, and he caught me at a bad moment. Afterward, I felt awful. So, I sat him down and apologized: "I'm sorry I snapped at you earlier. I was feeling frustrated, but that wasn't your fault. I should have handled it better." He immediately relaxed, and the tension melted away. He even gave me a hug, which, let's be honest, is rare for a 9-year-old boy. Modelling this kind of repair has made a huge difference in our family dynamic.

Why Your Brain Needs Downtime, Too

In a world where we're constantly juggling work, parenting, and life in general, it's easy to forget that our brains need rest, too. The constant stress of parenting can keep our **amygdala** on high alert, which makes it harder to stay calm and regulate our emotions. Taking time to recharge isn't just a luxury—it's essential for our mental health and our ability to be the calm, present parents we want to be.

Mom Hack (Prioritize Rest - Even When It Feels Impossible): I know, I know. Finding time to rest when you have kids feels like a joke. But even small moments of rest can make a big difference. I've started setting aside 10 minutes in the morning, before the chaos of the day begins, just to breathe, stretch, or have a quiet cup of tea. It's not a spa day, but it helps reset my brain and gives me a little buffer before the whirlwind starts.

Final Thoughts: You're the Calm in Their Storm

Parenting is messy, chaotic, and often overwhelming. But here's the thing: your calmness is your superpower. It's the anchor that helps regulate your kids' emotions and teaches them how to handle stress and frustration. And yes, there will be days when you feel anything but calm—days when you lose your cool, snap at your kids, or just want to crawl under the covers and hide. That's normal.

But the more we practice staying calm, the more we train our own brains to handle the chaos. And when we do lose it (because we will), we can always model how to repair and reconnect. Our kids don't need us to be perfect—they just need us to show up, breathe through the tough moments, and keep trying. After all, that's exactly what we're asking of them, too.

Conclusion: The Love of Parenting and Celebrating the Journey

Parenting is a wild, beautiful, exhausting, and incredibly rewarding journey. It's not about perfection, and it's certainly not about getting it all right every single time (because, let's be real, that's just not possible). It's about showing up, day after day, doing the best we can, and growing alongside our children. And if there's one thing I've learned from being a mother to three wonderfully unique kids, it's that they love us despite our imperfections, and we should love them for exactly who they are—not who we think they should be.

As parents, we spend so much time worrying about whether we're doing enough, whether we're present enough, whether we're giving our children everything they need. But let me tell you this: our kids will love us not for how many hours we spend with them or how perfect our parenting is, but for how much we show up with love, even on the tough days.

I know this because I've lived it. My three children—each so different and so special in their own ways—have been my greatest teachers. My 16-year-old, with her sharp wit and independence, shows me the power of curiosity and resilience. My 9-year-old, who can argue his way out of anything and question every rule, reminds me of the importance of critical thinking and standing up for what's right. And my 6-year-old, with his boundless energy and endless questions, teaches me to slow down and see the world through fresh eyes. They are the reason I find joy in the chaos, the heart behind everything I do.

Despite the fact that I run a school full-time, pursue my PhD in Brain-Based Learning and Teaching, and juggle all the demands that come with life, they love me for whatever time I can give them. And let me be honest—sometimes I'm not able to give them as much as I'd like. There are days when I'm tired, when the demands of work and study weigh on me, and when I feel like I'm not measuring up to the idea of "perfect parenting." But even on those days, they love me for showing up, for being their mom, and for simply being there, even if it's just for bedtime stories or a quick chat over dinner.

Our children don't need us to be perfect. They don't need us to always have the answers or to create a picture-perfect life for them. What they need is our presence, our love, and our willingness to be there—flawed and human—as they grow and learn. And just as their brains are developing and learning how to navigate the world, we too are constantly learning and evolving in our roles as parents.

So, to all the parents out there, remember this: your children will love you no matter your imperfections. They will remember the love you gave them, the moments of laughter, and the times you sat with them even when you were tired. And they will celebrate you for being their parent—the person who helps them navigate this big, messy, wonderful life.

Let's also celebrate our children for who they are, not who we expect them to be. Every child is unique, with their own strengths, quirks, and challenges. My kids have taught me that parenting isn't about shaping them into a version of ourselves or fulfilling our own expectations. It's about nurturing their uniqueness, celebrating their individual journeys, and loving them as they grow into the incredible people they are meant to be.

At the end of the day, parenting is a partnership—a journey of growth for both us and our children. We will make mistakes, we will have messy days, and we will question ourselves. But through it all, the love we share is what will carry us forward. So here's to the messy, joyful, chaotic, and deeply rewarding journey of parenthood. Let's embrace it, celebrate it, and continue growing alongside our children, with love as the guiding force every step of the way.

And as for my own kids—thank you for being patient with me as I juggle my career, my studies, and my role as your mom. You inspire me every day, and being your mother is the greatest joy of my life.

To all the parents reading this, remember: you are enough, just as you are. Your children love you, and you are doing an incredible job.

ABOUT THE AUTHOR

Shahista Ismail is an experienced educator with over 18 years of expertise in the field. She is the Founder Director of FloMont World School, where she integrates Montessori principles with Brain-Based research to foster engaging and nurturing learning environments for children. She is also the Co-Founder Director of the FMC training center, focusing on Teacher Training and Empowerment.

Shahista holds a Master's degree in Montessori Education from Sarasota University and is currently pursuing her PhD in Brain-Based Teaching from MLCU. As a mother of three, she draws on her personal experiences to offer practical, science-backed insights for parents navigating the complexities of raising Generation Alpha.

When not managing her school, conducting research, or parenting her own children, she dedicates her time to empowering other parents and educators, always with humor and warmth.

www.ingramcontent.com/pod-product-compliance
Lightning Source LLC
Chambersburg PA
CBHW021115130726

47988CB00003B/1031